Mind Matters:

Navigating the Landscape of Mental Well-Being

By

Robert T. Barner

TABLE OF CONTENT

INTRODUCTION

Mind Matters: Navigating the Landscape of Mental Well-Being" underlines the fundamental need to recognize and prioritize mental health. The reason is a vast and diverse landscape that impacts every part of our well-being, from our emotional resiliency to our interpersonal connections and general life pleasure.

Take a provocative trip across the complex mental landscape with "Mind Matters: Navigating the Landscape of Mental Well-Being." This fascinating investigation goes beyond the typical, beckoning you to investigate the intricate web of your feelings and ideas and the delicate equilibrium that shapes your mental health. It becomes critical to comprehend the complex terrain of our thoughts in a world where expectations and speed are constant. "Mind Matters" invites us to explore the intricacies that shape our emotional landscape, not simply a title.

We learn about the strength of our ideas, the shadows they throw, and the grit needed to keep things in balance as we make our way across the mental landscape.

This is not a solo voyage but a group exploration of the commonalities that unite us all. "Mind Matters" offers insights that explain the paths to mental resilience and emotional intelligence, acting as a compass for those searching for clarity.

Take a deep dive into "Mind Matters," where each chapter serves as a springboard for comprehending the subtleties of mental health. It is a story that goes beyond the clinical, combining elements of psychology, science, and personal histories to create a tapestry that speaks to the universal pulse of humanity. Both your intellect and the process of understanding its complexities are essential.

Are you prepared to traverse the terrain of your mental health? "Mind Matters" is what's in store for you—a journey that will change how you see, comprehend, and value the inviolability of your mind.

Definition of Mind Matters

Mind Matters highlights the relevance of the mind, covering cognitive processes, ideas, emotions, and mental states. It argues that mental well-being, psychological health, and cognitive functioning are vital to overall health and quality of life. The term may be used in numerous settings, such as raising mental health awareness, fostering mindfulness, or underlining the importance of psychological variables on behavior and decision-making.

In essence, Mind Matters stresses the necessity of paying attention to and prioritizing mental health and cognitive processes in all parts of life. This communicates that the condition of one's mind, including ideas, emotions, and mental well-being, is vital and substantially affects different aspects of life. It underlines the need to pay attention to and care for one's mental health, realizing that cognitive processes may impact general well-being, decision-making, and overall quality of life. This term typically emphasizes mindfulness, self-awareness, and the realization that our mental state influences our experiences and perceptions.

Mind Matters refers to the relevance and importance of the mind in numerous facets of life. It argues that the ideas, emotions, and cognitive processes within one's mind substantially influence personal well-being, decision-making, and general mental health.

The statement underlines that the mind is a significant component in controlling individual experiences and consequences.

Furthermore, this term implies the relevance or importance of mental processes, ideas, and emotions. It stresses the significance and effect of one's mentality, cognitive functions, and emotional well-being. The statement is commonly used to underline that what goes on in one's head is vital and can substantially affect numerous parts of life, such as decision-making, conduct, and general mental health.

Definition of Mental Well-being

Mental well-being, commonly called mental health or emotional well-being, is a complete and dynamic condition comprising an individual's emotional, psychological, and social health.

It is not just the absence of mental disease; it symbolizes a healthy and flourishing mental state. In this wide examination, we dig into the numerous dimensions of mental well-being, analyzing its different components, contributing factors, indications, and the problems individuals may encounter in sustaining good mental health. Additionally, I investigate techniques and behaviors that enhance and maintain mental well-being on personal and social levels.

Mental well-being is a comprehensive notion that incorporates the overall health of an individual's mind. It extends beyond the absence of mental diseases. It encompasses a condition of positive mental health where people can cope with life's usual demands, work effectively, and contribute to their communities.

CHAPTER 1

UNDERSTANDING THE MIND

Understanding the mind is a complicated and intriguing a task that involves several fields, including psychology, neuroscience, philosophy, and cognitive science. Here are some crucial factors to consider when investigating and trying to comprehend the mind:

Exploration of The Mind's Complexity

Examining the mind's complexity is a rich and nuanced a journey that entails deciphering the different levels and aspects of human awareness, cognition, and emotion.

Here are significant features demonstrating the intricacy of the mind:

Multifaceted Nature:

The word "multifaceted nature" refers to the numerous and complicated characteristics or features of a particular subject, concept, or phenomenon. It emphasizes that the issue has several sides or dimensions, and comprehending it requires evaluating various views or parts.

For example, a person's personality might be diverse since it contains many features, actions, and qualities.

The mind is not solitary but a complex interaction of many cognitive activities, emotions, memories, and sensations. Understanding the reason demands understanding its diverse nature and the complicated relationships between its components.

Unconscious Influences:

Much of the mind's activity happens at the unconscious level. Unconscious processes impact behavior, decision-making, and perceptions without someone's being completely aware of them. Exploring this secret dimension increases the knowledge of the mind's intricacy.

Unconscious impacts allude to the subtle and automatic effects that many circumstances might have on our ideas, feelings, and behaviors without our conscious knowledge. These impacts can arise from many sources, including prior experiences, cultural conditioning, social standards, and psychological processes.

Some instances of unintentional influences include:

➢ Implicit bias: unconscious attitudes or stereotypes that unintentionally impact our knowledge, behaviors, and decisions. These prejudices might be based on criteria such as race, gender, or socioeconomic class.

➢ Priming: activating particular thoughts or concepts in our minds, frequently without our knowledge, by exposure to specific stimuli. For instance, exposure to phrases connected to ageing could make someone walk more slowly without consciously understanding it.

➢ Social conditioning: unconscious acquisition of society norms, expectations, and actions without active awareness. This might include cultural influences, familial background, and societal expectations that impact our thoughts and actions.

➢ Emotional Contagion: unconsciously taking up and mimicking the emotions of others around us. This can lead to the propagation of emotions within a group, even without explicit communication.

➢ Selective Perception: unconsciously filtering information depending on our previous beliefs, expectations, and experiences. This can result in skewed interpretations of events.

Understanding and becoming aware of these unconscious impacts is vital for personal development, successful communication, and making informed decisions.

Techniques such as mindfulness, self-reflection, and diversity. Proper training can assist individuals in developing a greater level of awareness regarding these matters and lessen their potential detrimental impact.

Individual Variability

Every individual's mind is unique, molded by genetics, experiences, and environmental circumstances. The variety in personality, cognitive aptitude and emotional reactions add complexity to the study of the mind.

Individual variability refers to the inherent variances and diversity among individuals within a community or group.

This notion emphasizes that people are unique and can differ in different characteristics, including features, abilities, interests, and actions. Understanding individual variability is vital in psychology, education, healthcare, and business.

Here are some significant points relating to individual variability:

• Personality: Individuals display a wide range of personality qualities. Personality traits include extroversion, openness, conscientiousness, agreeableness, and emotional stability. These features contribute to the individuality of individuals and determine how they interact with the environment.

• Cognitive talents: People differ in cognitive skills, including intellect, problem-solving ability, and creativity. Recognizing these variances is vital in education and the business to accommodate varied learning styles and techniques.

• Learning ways: Individuals have varied interests and methods of learning. Some may favor visual learning, while others may thrive in aural or tactile learning. Tailoring educational procedures to meet various learning styles might enhance the learning experience.

• Cultural Background: Cultural variety leads to individual variability. Cultural elements such as beliefs, conventions, and communication styles impact individuals' viewpoints and behaviors. Understanding and accepting cultural differences is vital for good communication and collaboration.

• Biological Factors: Genetic variances lead to disparities in physical features, health issues, and susceptibility to specific diseases. Individual reactions to drugs and environmental circumstances can also differ based on genetic composition.

• Emotional Responses: People display varied emotional responses to circumstances affected by prior experiences, temperament, and coping techniques. Recognizing and comprehending these variances is vital in the mental health and therapy sectors.

• Interests and Hobbies: Individuals have distinct interests, passions, and hobbies that contribute to their personality. Recognizing and accepting these differences produces a more inclusive and supportive atmosphere.

Acknowledging and accepting individual variability is vital for encouraging diversity and inclusion, adapting treatments to match individual needs, and building a more nuanced understanding of human behavior in varied circumstances. It also stresses the necessity of avoiding prejudices and acknowledging the richness of diversity among individuals.

Emotional Depth

Emotional depth refers to the richness, complexity, and intensity of an individual's emotional experiences. It argues that emotions are not simple or one-dimensional but may be complex, profound, and impacted by various events. People with emotional depth generally have a heightened awareness of their own emotions and the emotions of others, and they may engage with their feelings in a more complex and nuanced manner. Here are some significant features of emotional depth:

• Complexity of Emotions: Emotions are not always clear; they can be nuanced and comprise a mix of sensations. Someone with emotional depth could feel emotions that are multifaceted and interrelated.

• Self-awareness: Individuals with emotional depth tend to have high self-awareness. They comprehend their emotional states, can explain their sentiments, and ponder on the underlying reasons for their emotions.

• Empathy: Emotional depth frequently implies a heightened ability for empathy. People with this attribute may thoroughly comprehend and connect with the feelings of others, acknowledging and respecting the complexity of differing views.

• Expression of Vulnerability: Emotional depth may be connected with a readiness to express vulnerability. This involves being upfront about one's challenges, anxieties, and vulnerabilities and building authentic and meaningful connections with others.

Emotions are deep and diverse experiences that add to the

richness of the human mind. The complexity of emotions rests in their subjective character, the interplay between different emotions, and their effect on decision-making and behavior.

Developing emotional depth is a dynamic and continuing process that might entail self-reflection, investigation of one's emotional environment, and a willingness to interact with pleasant and negative feelings.

It contributes to a more honest and meaningful existence, encouraging more significant relationships and a more profound knowledge of oneself and others.

Cognitive Processes

Cognitive functions such as perception, attention, memory, problem-solving, and many more are essential to the mind's complexity. The reason effortlessly blends various processes to traverse the world, solve issues, and make judgments.

Here are some critical cognitive processes:

• Perception: Perception includes the interpretation of sensory information from the environment. It involves seeing, hearing, touching, tasting, and smelling. Perception helps humans make sense of the world around them.

• Attention: Attention is focusing on particular stimuli while disregarding others. It is vital for picking up relevant information for subsequent processing. Depending on the work, attention can be selective, sustained, or split.

• Memory: Memory includes the storing and retrieval of information. It is generally separated into multiple forms, including sensory memory, short-term memory, and long-term

memory. Memory operations include encoding (input of information), storage (retaining information), and retrieval (retrieving stored information).

• Language Processing: Language is a complicated cognitive process involving understanding and producing speech or written material. This includes comprehending syntax, semantics, and pragmatics. Language processing also involves reading and writing skills.

• Learning: Learning is acquiring new information or abilities via experience, study, or teaching. Cognitive processes such as encoding, rehearsal, and consolidation play a part in learning. Learning can be implicit (unconscious) or explicit (conscious).

• Problem-solving: Problem-solving is finding solutions to difficulties or impediments. It often involves mental activities such as describing the problem, developing possible solutions, assessing options, and applying solutions.

• Decision-making: Decision-making entails picking a plan of action from several choices. Cognitive biases, heuristics, and rational decision-making processes can impact it. Emotional and social variables may also play a role.

• Reasoning: Reasoning is the capacity to think and generate conclusions based on available facts. Deductive reasoning entails moving from basic principles to particular cases, whereas inductive reasoning involves deriving general principles from specific instances.

• Executive Functions: Executive functions are higher-order cognitive processes that involve abilities such as planning, organization, cognitive flexibility, and self-control. The prefrontal cortex is related to these functions of the brain.

• Problem-solving: Problem-solving is finding solutions to difficulties or impediments. It often involves mental activities such as describing the problem, developing possible solutions, assessing options, and applying solutions.

Developmental Changes

The mind experiences significant developmental changes throughout its lifespan. From the early stages of infancy to the intricacies of adult cognition, knowing how the mind changes adds depth to examining its complexity.

These changes can involve different dimensions, including

physical, cognitive, emotional and social development. Developmental psychology focuses on researching these changes and understanding the variables that drive them.

Here are essential points relating to developmental changes:

• Physical Development: This encompasses changes in the body, such as growth, motor abilities, and changes in organ systems. It encompasses physical growth from birth to adulthood and changes in physical ability and health throughout the lifespan.

• Cognitive Development: Cognitive development relates to changes in intellectual capacities, including thinking, reasoning, problem-solving, memory, and language learning.

• Emotional growth: Emotional growth encompasses changes in how individuals feel, express, and regulate emotions. It encompasses the development of emotional awareness, knowledge, and the ability to control and express emotions in a socially appropriate manner.

• Social Development: Social development refers to changes in how individuals interact with others and perceive the social world. This encompasses developing social skills, connections, and an awareness of social norms and roles.

• Identity Formation: Identity formation is critical to adolescence and early adulthood. It entails investigating and constructing a sense of self, including one's values, beliefs, and life objectives.

• Puberty and Adolescence: Puberty is a stage of physical development defined by hormonal changes that lead to sexual maturity. Adolescence is a more significant phase spanning physical, cognitive, and social development, frequently marked by a desire for identity and growing independence.

Interaction with the Environment

The mind is not solitary but continually interacts with the surroundings. External inputs, cultural influences, and social interactions alter cognitive processes and contribute to the intricate fabric of the mind's complexity.

Interaction with the environment is a dynamic and reciprocal interaction between individuals and their external environments, significantly determining growth and behavior.

This interaction involves the interplay of genetic and environmental variables, impacting cognitive, emotional, and social development. Environmental enrichment, stressors, cultural influences, social learning, and the biopsychosocial model all contribute to this connection. Recognizing the relevance of a person's fit with their surroundings and addressing more significant problems like sustainability are vital factors.

The Mind-Body Connection

The mind and body, inextricably interwoven, constitute a deep and symbiotic interaction that defines our well-being. This physiological relationship extends to emotions, thinking, and general health. This investigation of the mind-body link reveals the delicate dance that characterizes our holistic life.

1. Understanding the Unity:

The mind-body link is not a notion; it's the substance of our existence. At its essence, this link represents the interconnectedness of mental and physical health. Our ideas and emotions affect our physical condition; conversely, our physical well-being impacts our mental state. To comprehend one, we must appreciate the other.

2. The Power of Thoughts:

Our ideas are more than transitory happenings; they significantly influence physical health. Positive thoughts may initiate a cascade of neurochemical reactions that raise mood and increase general well-being.

Conversely, persistent stress or negative thinking patterns may emerge physiologically, harming immunological function, cardiovascular health, and digestive systems.

3. Emotions as Messengers:

Emotions, sometimes called the language of the soul, are strong messages that cross the gap between mind and body. When we experience emotions, our body reacts with physiological changes. Stress, for instance, promotes the release of cortisol, influencing heart rate and blood pressure. Understanding and controlling emotions is crucial to preserving balance within the mind-body relationship.

4. Stress and Relaxation Response:

The omnipresent presence of stress in everyday life highlights the relevance of the mind-body link. Chronic stress not only burdens mental health but also manifests physically, leading to illnesses including muscular tightness, migraines, and reduced immunological function.

Conversely, triggering the relaxation response via meditation and deep breathing supports physical and mental renewal.

5. Lifestyle Choices and Physical Health:

Daily choices, from diet to physical exercise, have a key influence on the mind-body link. A healthy diet feeds the body and brain, impacting cognitive performance and emotional well-being. Regular exercise strengthens the body and produces endorphins, the body's natural mood enhancers.

6. The Role of Mind-Body Practices:

Mind-body activities, ranging from yoga to mindfulness meditation, provide purposeful paths for developing harmony. These activities actively engage the mind and body, fostering relaxation, stress reduction, and heightened self-awareness. They become vehicles for better understanding the mind-body link and supporting general well-being.

7. Holistic Wellness:

In essence, the mind-body link underlines the comprehensive aspect of well-being. To obtain actual health, one must treat not just bodily problems but also dig into the realms of mental and emotional well-being. This holistic approach highlights the interdependence of all elements of our lives and encourages people to engage in their health journey actively.

As we travel the many paths of the mind-body connection, let us embrace the deep truth that our well-being is a harmonic symphony, where the mind and body dance together perfectly. This inquiry urges us to comprehend and actively foster this link, unleashing the possibility for robust health and deep self-awareness.

The Connection Between Mental and Physical Health

Maintaining good physical health is closely linked to mental well-being and vice versa.

It is essential to recognize the strong connection between the two and take steps to care for both aspects

of our health. It is necessary to understand that mental well-being affects physical health and vice versa. Therefore, maintaining a balance between them is crucial for leading a healthy and fulfilling life.

Numerous studies demonstrate that mental and physical well-being are tightly interwoven, impacting each other in multiple ways.

• Biological Basis: The brain and body connect via a complex network of neurotransmitters and hormones. Imbalances in these substances may impact both mental and physical health.

• Stress Response: Mental stress may generate some physical responses due to certain stimuli, including an elevated heart rate, increased blood pressure, and other reactions—changes in the immune system. Chronic stress is connected to different health concerns.

- Psychosomatic Effects: Mental health disorders may appear physically. For example, depression may lead to weariness, changes in appetite, and sleep difficulties.

- Lifestyle Factors: Healthy lifestyle choices, like regular exercise and a balanced diet, boost physical health and benefit mental well-being.

- Chronic Illness and Mental Health: Chronic physical ailments may lead to mental health concerns, and vice versa. Managing one component typically implies addressing the other.

- Mind-Body Therapies: Practices like meditation, yoga, and mindfulness have been demonstrated to have good impacts on both mental and physical health.

- Inflammation and Mental Health: Inflammatory processes in the body are connected to many mental health disorders. Conditions like depression have been related to elevated levels of inflammation.

- Social Connection: Social support and strong interactions contribute to mental and physical well-being. Isolation and loneliness, on the other hand, may badly damage both.

- Health Behaviors: Mental health may affect health habits such as drug use, sleep patterns, and adherence to medical recommendations, influencing overall physical health.

Understanding and managing the interrelated nature of mental and physical health is vital for holistic healthcare and well-being.

Consciousness and Self-Awareness

The nature of awareness itself is a significant part of the mind's complexity. Exploring how humans become aware of their existence, thoughts, and experiences adds depth to understanding the mind. Consciousness and self-awareness are crucial to the human intellect.

Consciousness encompasses awareness of ideas, feelings, and the environment across multiple stages, from alertness to altered consciousness.

Self-awareness is the recognition of one's thoughts and identity. Metacognition includes comprehending thinking processes, while mindfulness cultivates present awareness.

The stream of consciousness depicts the dynamic character of thinking. Altered states, neurology, and the experience of agency add to our knowledge. These themes span psychology, neurology, and philosophy, affecting human growth and interpersonal interactions.

CHAPTER 2

UNDERSTANDING MENTAL WELL-BEING

The World Health Organization describes mental health as "a state of well-being where individuals can realize their abilities, manage the normal stresses of life, work productively and efficiently, and contribute to their community."

Components of Mental Well-being

- Mind-Body Connection: A fundamental part of mental well-being is realizing the deep relationship between the mind and body. The mind-body link highlights that psychological and physical health are interrelated; changes in one area can impact the other. Practices such as mindfulness, meditation, and exercise increase this connection, generating a comprehensive feeling of well-being.

- Emotional Resilience: Emotional resilience is a cornerstone of mental well-being, representing the ability to adapt to and bounce back from life's hardships.

Individuals with great emotional resilience can endure challenges, failures, and adversities while retaining a positive outlook and emotional balance.

- Psychological Health: Psychological health comprises self-esteem, self-acceptance, and a feeling of purpose. It entails understanding and embracing oneself, acknowledging strengths and flaws, and fostering a pleasant psychological state that adds to general well-being.

- Social connectivity: Human beings are fundamentally social animals, and social connectivity is a key component of mental well-being. Developing and nurturing strong connections with family, friends, and the community can profoundly impact one's emotional and psychological wellness.

When we feel connected and supported by those around us, we experience a sense of belonging and security that can help us easily navigate life's ups and downs.

For example, having a close relationship with a family member or friend can provide a safe space to express our thoughts and feelings, receive constructive feedback, and feel heard and understood.

Similarly, being involved in our community through volunteering, participating in events, or joining groups can give us a sense of purpose and fulfillment while also providing opportunities to meet new people and expand our social network. These positive interactions can help us maintain a healthy mindset and improve our well-being.

• Balanced Emotions: A fundamental sign of mental well-being is the capacity to detect, analyze, and regulate a range of emotions. This entails fostering emotional intelligence and resilience, enabling individuals to respond adaptively to varied, dynamic events.

Importance of Mental Well-Being

Mental well-being is vital for general health and quality of life.

Here are a few reasons showing its importance:

1. Emotional Stability:

Mental well-being helps to emotional stability, enabling individuals to better cope with life's difficulties and pressures.

It helps individuals to handle emotions successfully and have a happy viewpoint. Emotional stability is the capacity to control and regulate emotions properly.

Individuals with high mental well-being are better suited to handle stress, anxiety, and other emotional issues without becoming overwhelmed. Emotional stability helps to a more balanced and robust reaction to life's ups and downs, encouraging a sense of control and consistency in one's emotional life.

2. Physical Health:

Mental and physical wellness have a strong correlation and are closely related. Good mental well-being can significantly the immune system, cardiovascular health, and general body processes. The mind and body are interrelated, and mental well-being can impact physical health.

Chronic stress and mental health concerns can contribute to many physical health problems, including cardiovascular troubles, impaired immune systems and other disorders.

Prioritizing mental well-being via techniques like mindfulness and stress reduction can benefit physical health and longevity.

3. Productivity:

A healthy mind promotes cognitive function, focus, and problem-solving ability. Individuals with strong mental well-being are frequently more productive at work and in their everyday activities. Mental well-being is intimately connected to cognitive function.

Individuals who are mentally healthy can think more clearly, focus on tasks and solve issues successfully. Employers are realizing the significance of mental well-being in the workplace, establishing measures to assist employee mental health, leading to higher productivity and job satisfaction.

4. Relationships:

Mental well-being is critical in creating and maintaining good relationships. It enhances efficient communication, empathy and understanding, which are crucial for good interpersonal interactions. Healthy relationships involve excellent communication, empathy and compassion. Mental well-being contributes to emotional intelligence, boosting the capacity to manage and maintain relationships.

Individuals with robust mental health can better assist others and sustain positive connections, forming a helpful social network.

5. Resilience:

People with strong mental well-being are frequently more resilient in facing adversities. They can bounce back from failures, adjust to changes, and keep a sense of control over their life.

Resilience is the capacity to bounce back from hardship. Good mental well-being creates resilience, enabling individuals to endure challenges, adapt to change and learn from failures.

Resilient individuals are more prone to perceive setbacks as chances for progress rather than insurmountable hurdles.

6. Quality of Life:

Mental well-being significantly improves an individual's overall quality of life. It impacts how one experiences and views life, impacting personal satisfaction and happiness. Mental well-being is crucial to an individual's overall quality of life. It changes how one experiences and views life events, leading to a sense of fulfilment, purpose, and life happiness.

Activities that improve mental well-being include engaging in leisure activities, dedicating time to one's family and friends, and cherishing moments spent with loved ones. Practicing self-care boosts the overall quality of life.

7. Prevention of Mental Health Disorders:

Maintaining mental well-being is vital for preventing the development of mental health issues. It entails establishing positive behaviors, managing stress, and getting assistance when required.

Proactive efforts to preserve mental well-being, such as stress management, seeking social support, and adopting good lifestyle choices, can contribute to preventing the emergence of mental health illnesses. Early intervention and understanding play a critical role in treating possible mental health difficulties before they worsen.

8. Community Well-Being:

Maintaining well-being is paramount and crucial in communities and societies. It is essential to prioritize and support mental health in order to ensure a healthy and thriving society.

Societies emphasizing mental health tend to be more supportive, inclusive, and resilient. The mental well-being of people collectively contributes to the well-being of communities and organizations.

Communities that value mental health are frequently more supportive, inclusive, and resilient in facing adversity. Social initiatives, community participation, and destigmatization activities help to build circumstances that encourage mental well-being at a more significant societal level.

9. Educational Attainment:

Mental well-being is connected to academic performance. Students with robust mental health are likelier to participate in learning, do well academically, and fulfil their educational goals. Mental well-being is connected to educational performance.

Psychologically healthy students are more likely to be engaged in learning, attend school regularly, and perform well academically. Educational institutions are realizing the necessity of mental health support services to guarantee the well-being of students, establishing settings conducive to learning.

Generally, enhancing mental well-being takes a comprehensive strategy incorporating life's physical, emotional, and social components. It is a continual process that involves self-care, social support, and a pleasant atmosphere.

Factors affecting Mental well-being

Several aspects affect mental health, encompassing. It is an intricate combination of biological, psychological, social, and environmental elements.

Here are some fundamental aspects that might improve mental wellbeing:

1. Biological Factors:

• Genetics: Genetic factors contribute to an individual's propensity to certain mental health concerns. A family history of mental issues can heighten the risk.

• Brain Chemistry: Neurotransmitters and imbalances in brain chemicals impact mental wellness.

Abnormalities in neurotransmitter activity could also contribute to disorders like sorrow or anxiety.

2. Psychological Factors:

• Cognitive Patterns: Negative ideas, warped thinking, and maladaptive cognitive processes can impair mental health. Cognitive behavioral therapy (CBT) seeks to address and modify these patterns.

• Personality qualities: Certain personality features may raise the chance of mental health disorders. For example, perfectionism or poor self-esteem could contribute to conditions like obsessive-compulsive disorder or depression.

3. Lifestyle Factors:

• Physical Health: Physical and mental health are interrelated and can greatly affect each other. Conditions, including chronic disease, substance usage, or lack of exercise, might impair mental well-being.

• Sleep habits: Disrupted sleep habits or insufficient sleep can cause mental health challenges, including mood disorders and cognitive impairments.

• Nutrition: Diet and nutritional factors might alter mental health. Nutrient shortages or imbalances may lead to numerous mental health issues.

4. Trauma & Stress:

• Traumatic Events: Exposure to trauma, such as violence, accidents or natural disasters can have a considerable effect on mental health, resulting in diseases like post-traumatic stress disorder (PTSD).

• Chronic Stress: Persistent stressors, such as work-related stress, financial obstacles, or interpersonal problems, may exacerbate or promote the development of mental health issues through certain factors.

5. Cultural and Societal influences:

• Cultural Norms: Cultural factors affect attitudes towards mental health, stigma, and help-seeking practices. Cultural sensitivity is crucial for excellent mental health care.

• Discrimination and Marginalization: Experiences of discrimination, prejudice, or marginalization based on factors like race, gender, or sexual orientation can profoundly impair mental health.

Indicators of Good Mental Well-being

• Positive Relationships: Building and keeping strong connections with others is a major predictor of high mental well-being. Effective communication and reciprocal support within relationships contribute to emotional and psychological well-being.

- Resilience in Adversity: The capacity to overcome setbacks and obstacles with strength indicates high mental well-being. Individuals who can learn and grow through hardship display a good cognitive approach.

- Emotional Regulation: Effectively controlling and expressing emotions without being overwhelmed by them is important to mental well-being. Positively coping with stress adds to emotional resilience.

- Purpose and Meaning: Purpose and direction in life are related to high mental well-being. Pursuing meaningful objectives and engaging in activities that create fulfillment contribute to overall psychological wellness.

- Self-Acceptance: Embracing oneself with strengths and shortcomings is a basic part of excellent mental well-being. Positive self-esteem and a healthy self-concept contribute to psychological resilience.

Challenges to Mental Well-being

- Stigma: Social stigma around mental health disorders might inhibit open talks and seeking assistance. Promoting awareness and decreasing stigma is vital for building an atmosphere that fosters mental well-being.

- Access to services: Disparities in access to mental health services, including treatment and support, pose difficulties to mental well-being. Advocating for equal access to mental health care is vital for tackling this situation.

- Stress and Burnout: High chronic stress and burnout levels, frequently linked with modern lives, can affect mental well-being. Prioritizing self-care and stress management measures is vital for sustaining excellent mental health.

- Unhealthy Coping techniques: Dependence on drugs, avoidance habits, or other harmful coping strategies may negatively affect mental health. Encouraging the development of good coping techniques is vital for promoting mental well-being.

Promoting Healthy Mental Well-being

• Self-Care Practices: Prioritizing self-care, including enough rest, leisure activities, and relaxation, is vital for boosting mental well-being. Recognizing and addressing personal needs contribute to overall emotional and psychological wellness.

• Open Communication: Fostering open talks about mental health is crucial for fostering well-being. Creating a friendly atmosphere for expressing thoughts and seeking assistance helps a good mental health culture.

• Community Engagement: Participating in community activities and creating social relationships increase the sense of belonging and support. A robust communal network is important for overall mental wellbeing.

• Seeking Professional Help: Recognizing when further assistance is necessary and seeking professional help is a proactive step toward sustaining mental well-being. Removing obstacles to accessing mental health services is vital for guaranteeing timely support.

In conclusion, mental well-being is a holistic and dynamic condition that comprises emotional resilience, psychological health, and social connectivity.

Several variables impact it, including genetics, environment, lifestyle choices, and life experiences. Indicators of healthy mental well-being include meaningful connections, perseverance in adversity, emotional control, a feeling of purpose, and self-acceptance.

Challenges such as stigma, restricted access to services, stress, and poor coping techniques can influence mental well-being.

However, supporting mental well-being via self-care routines, open communication, community participation, and seeking professional treatment adds to a good mental health culture.

Embracing a comprehensive approach to mental well-being is not only a personal initiative but a social commitment to create a society that appreciates and promotes the mental health of its people.

Impact of lifestyle on mental wellbeing

Lifestyle choices and behaviors have a vital impact on shaping mental well-being. How people live their lives, including their daily routines, food choices, physical exercise, and stress management, may dramatically influence mental health.

Here's a summary of the essential factors of how lifestyle might impact mental wellbeing:

1. Physical Activity:

• Positive Impact: Regular exercise has been related to increased mood, decreased symptoms of anxiety and depression, and excellent cognitive performance. Exercise releases endorphins, which are neurotransmitters that function as natural mood boosters.

• Negative Impact: Sedentary lifestyles, typified by a lack of physical exercise, are connected with a greater incidence of sadness and anxiety. Insufficient exercise might lead to elevated stress levels.

2. Nutrition:

• Positive Impact: A well-balanced and healthy diet supplies critical nutrients that enhance brain function. Omega-3 fatty acids, vitamins, and minerals support mental well-being.

• Negative Impact: Poor nutrition, notably diets heavy in processed foods and sweets, is associated with an increased risk of mental health issues. Nutrient shortages may impair mood, cognition, and general brain function.

3. Sleep Hygiene:

• Positive Impact: Quality sleep is vital for mental

wellbeing. Establishing appropriate sleep hygiene habits, such as keeping a regular sleep schedule and having a pleasant sleep environment, may enhance mood and cognitive performance.

• Negative Impact: Sleep disruptions, including insomnia and irregular sleep patterns, are associated with increased risk. Mood disorders, such as sadness and anxiety, can significantly impact a person's emotional state.

4. Stress Management:

• Positive Impact: Effective stress management practices, such as mindfulness, meditation, and relaxation exercises, may lower stress hormones and increase mental well-being.

• Negative Impact: Chronic stress, originating from causes such as job pressure, financial problems, or interpersonal disputes, is a substantial risk factor for the development of mental health difficulties.

5. Social Connections:

• strong Impact: Strong social support and strong social

ties lead to emotional well-being. Engaging in meaningful social connections may create a sense of belonging, which is essential as it can help to alleviate feelings of loneliness.

• Negative Impact: Social isolation and loneliness increase the risk of mental health problems. Addressing these issues and seeking support from loved ones or mental health professionals is essential. Lack of social support might lead to feelings of despair and anxiety.

6. Substance Use:

• Positive Impact: Avoiding drug addiction or excessive alcohol intake helps mental health. Substance-free lives lead to more excellent cognitive performance and emotional well-being.

• Negative Impact: Substance misuse, including alcohol and illicit substances, is connected with an increased risk of mental health issues and may aggravate existing symptoms.

7. Work-Life Balance:

• Positive Impact: Balancing work and personal life, establishing boundaries, and taking breaks lead to decreased stress and enhanced mental well-being.

• Negative influence: High levels of work-related stress, lengthy working hours, and a lack of balance may lead to burnout and severely influence mental health.

8. Mindfulness and Relaxation:

• Positive Impact: Mindfulness meditation and relaxation methods may help manage stress, develop self-awareness, and improve general mental well-being.

• Negative Impact: Neglecting self-care and relaxation may add to feelings of overload and adversely influence mental health.

Adopting a comprehensive and healthy lifestyle that includes frequent physical exercise, a balanced diet, appropriate sleep, and efficient stress management is crucial to sustaining mental well-being. Making healthy lifestyle choices can decrease the likelihood of mental health issues and improve overall well-being. Additionally, obtaining professional treatment when required is vital for resolving mental health difficulties.

CHAPTER 3
EMBRACING EMOTIONAL INTELLIGENCE

Definition and Significance of Emotional Intelligence

Definition of Emotional Intelligence (EI): Emotional Intelligence refers to the ability to recognize, understand, and manage our emotions and those of others. It involves identifying different emotions accurately and responding appropriately to them in different situations. Developing emotional Intelligence can help individuals build stronger relationships, improve communication skills, and enhance their overall well-being. It encompasses skills and competencies that help individuals navigate social relationships, empathize with others, manage their feelings, and make educated decisions based on emotional information.

Components of Emotional Intelligence:

1. Self-awareness: Recognizing and comprehending one's feelings, strengths, flaws, values, and motives.

2. Self-Regulation: Managing and managing one's emotions, impulses, and reactions in diverse situations.

3. Motivation: Being driven by internal objectives, having a passion for one's profession, and continuing in the face of failures.

4. Empathy: Understanding and sharing the feelings of others, acknowledging their views, and reacting with compassion.

5. Social Skills: Effectively navigating social settings, creating and sustaining strong connections, and communicating with others.

Significance of Emotional Intelligence

1. Enhanced Interpersonal connections: Individuals with

high emotional Intelligence are more prepared to comprehend the feelings of others, leading to more excellent communication,

conflict resolution, and the formation of good interpersonal connections.

2. Effective Leadership: Emotional Intelligence is vital
to effective leadership. Leaders with high EI may inspire and encourage their people, overcome hurdles, and establish a favorable work atmosphere.

3. Disagreement Resolution: Individuals with vital
emotional Intelligence may handle disputes more successfully by recognizing the emotions behind the disagreement, controlling their emotional responses, and finding solutions considering all parties' feelings.

4. Adaptability: Emotional Intelligence helps individuals
to adjust to changing situations and handle stress and uncertainty more successfully. It requires adaptability, resilience, and openness to new ideas and viewpoints.

5. Improved Communication: People with strong emotional Intelligence are good communicators. They can convey their views and feelings effectively, listen attentively to others, and change their communication style to diverse audiences.

6. Decision-Making: Emotional Intelligence leads to better decision-making by incorporating emotional information into the decision-making process. It helps individuals analyze the emotional effect of choices and make decisions that accord with their beliefs.

7. Personal Wellbeing: Individuals with vital emotional Intelligence tend to have higher mental health and well-being. They can negotiate life's problems with greater Resilience, retain an optimistic attitude, and establish a supportive social network.

8. Team Collaboration: Emotional Intelligence enhances collaboration and cooperation in team contexts. Team members

who understand and accept one another's emotions may work together more successfully and establish a healthy team culture.

9. Conflict Prevention: Emotional Intelligence may contribute to reducing disputes by increasing open communication, empathy, and a pleasant emotional environment within relationships and organizations.

In essence, emotional Intelligence is a significant set of talents that increases numerous aspects of personal and professional life. It leads to successful communication, pleasant relationships, and general well-being, making it a crucial determinant in individual and societal success.

Developing and improving Emotional Intelligence

Developing and increasing emotional intelligence (EI) is a lifetime process that requires self-awareness, self-reflection, and purposeful practice. Here are practical techniques to improve and enhance emotional Intelligence:

1. Self-Awareness:

Reflection: Regularly reflect on your emotions, identifying and acknowledging them without judgment. Consider how your emotions impact your ideas and activities.

Journaling: Keep a diary to document your emotional experiences, triggers, and patterns. This helps you acquire insights into reoccurring emotional responses.

2. Self-Regulation:

Mindfulness and Meditation: Practice mindfulness to stay present and improve self-regulation. Meditation practices can assist in managing stress and increase emotional Resilience.

Deep Breathing: Engage in deep-breathing exercises to relax the nervous system and manage emotional reactions, especially during periods of stress.

3. Motivation:

Goal Setting: Set relevant and realistic objectives to keep motivated. Align your dreams with your beliefs, producing a feeling of purpose and enthusiasm.

Positive Affirmations: Use positive affirmations to keep a positive mentality and enhance motivation. Focus on your talents and successes.

4. Empathy:

Active Listening: Practice active listening to grasp others' viewpoints fully. Avoid interrupting and affirming their emotions and expressing empathy.

Perspective-Taking: Put yourself in others' position to comprehend their feelings and intentions. Consider various ideas to extend your outlook.

5. Social Skills:

Effective Communication: Develop precise and aggressive communication abilities. Be observant of non-verbal indicators, such as body language and facial expressions, to strengthen interpersonal relationships.

Conflict Resolution: Learn and apply practical conflict

resolution approaches. Focus on creating mutually beneficial solutions and sustaining positive connections.

6. Continuous Learning:

Seek input: Solicit input from others regarding your emotional Intelligence. This outsider perspective can bring valuable insights and opportunities for growth.

Educate Yourself: Read books, take workshops, and explore resources on Emotional Intelligence to improve your understanding and perfect your talents.

7. Cultivate Resilience:

Learn from Setbacks: View obstacles and setbacks as chances for progress. Analyze how you respond to hardship and discover development opportunities.

Optimistic Self-Talk: Develop a happy and resilient mentality. Challenge negative self-talk and focus on solutions rather than concentrating on issues.

8. Relationship Building:

Networking: Actively engage in networking and create varied ties. This broadens your social abilities and exposes you to diverse ideas.

Team Collaboration: Participate in group activities to develop your capacity to work cooperatively and understand group dynamics.

Remember that building emotional Intelligence is a slow and continual process. Consistent work and a dedication to self-improvement are vital. Adopting these tactics into everyday life may create greater emotional Intelligence, improve personal and professional relationships, and increase decision-making and overall well-being.

Emotional control and its impact on mental health

Emotional regulation is the capacity to successfully

regulate and modulate one's emotional responses in diverse settings. It entails recognizing, interpreting, and influencing emotions to maintain a good emotional balance.

The impact of emotional control on mental health is profound and multifaceted:

1. Stress Reduction

- Impact: Effective emotional control helps lessen stress's physiological and psychological effects. By controlling pressure, individuals can prevent the accumulation of chronic stress, which is associated with numerous mental health concerns.

2. Improved Mood and Wellbeing

- Impact: Managing emotions helps to create a more happy and stable mood. It allows individuals to manage daily problems without being overwhelmed by negative feelings.

3. Enhanced Interpersonal Relationships

- Impact: Emotional control plays a critical role in interpersonal relations. It helps individuals express themselves responsibly, sympathize with others, and negotiate situations efficiently.

4. Resilience and Coping:

- Impact: Emotional control leads to Resilience, the ability to bounce back from adversity. It allows individuals to manage obstacles, failures, and life pressures more efficiently.

5. Reduced Risk of Mental Health Disorders:

- Impact: Effective emotional control is related to a decreased chance of developing mental health problems, including anxiety, depression, and mood disorders.

6. Cognitive Functioning:

- Impact: Emotional control promotes cognitive functioning, including attention, memory, and decision-making. It enables individuals to think more clearly and make educated choices.

7. Emotional Intelligence:

- Impact: Emotional regulation is an essential component of emotional Intelligence.

Individuals with vital emotional Intelligence can navigate social circumstances, comprehend others' feelings, and form compassionate relationships.

8. Decreased Risk of Substance Abuse:

- Impact: Effective emotional regulation minimizes the chance of resorting to substances (alcohol, drugs) as a maladaptive coping technique for emotional pain.

9. Positive Impact on Physical Health:

- Impact: Emotional management has physiological effects on the body, including lower levels of stress hormones and increased immunological function.

In summary, emotional regulation is a vital component of mental health. Its influence spans numerous areas, impacting mood, relationships, Resilience, and general well-being. Developing and improving emotional regulation skills is essential to supporting mental health and maintaining a balanced and meaningful existence.

CHAPTER 4

COPING WITH STRESS AND ANXIETY

Understanding Stress

Stress is a typical emotional and physical reaction to situations that demand a response. It is a natural mechanism that prepares us to confront challenges or threats. It can be triggered by various factors such as work, relationships, or financial issues. Stress can manifest in different ways, including physical symptoms like headaches, muscle tension, and stomach problems; many people experience not only physical signs but also emotional symptoms such as anxiety, irritability, and depression.

Managing stress effectively is essential to maintain good mental and physical health. The body's normal reaction to events necessitates adjustment or adaptation.

While moderate stress may motivate and help individuals tackle difficulties, excessive or chronic stress can harm physical and mental well-being.

Key Components of Stress

1. Stressors: These events or conditions activate the stress reaction. Stressors can be external (e.g., job deadlines, financial

obligations) or internal (e.g., negative thoughts, self-imposed pressure).

2. The stress reaction: When presented with a stressor, the body starts the "fight or flight" reaction, releasing hormones like cortisol and adrenaline. When we perceive danger, our body undergoes physiological changes to prepare itself to respond.

3. Short-Term vs. Chronic Stress: Short-term stress can be adaptive, helping individuals cope with urgent obstacles. However, chronic stress, which continues over a lengthy period, can lead to physical and mental health difficulties.

4. Individual Responses: Responses to stress vary significantly among people. Heredity, coping methods, and resilience impact how individuals perceive and handle stress.

Types of Stress

Stress is a complicated and diverse phenomenon that can emerge in numerous forms. Different sorts of stress can harm persons physically, emotionally, and psychologically. Here are some common forms of stress:

1. Acute Stress:

• Description: Acute stress is short-term and arises from recent demands or pressures. It is a normal and essential response that may be inspiring.

Example: The stress of studying for an exam or reaching a tight deadline.

2. Chronic Stress:

• Description: Chronic stress is long-term and frequently continues over a prolonged period. It might stem from persistent life problems or unresolved severe stress.

Example: Prolonged financial troubles, continuing work-related issues, or chronic relationship obstacles.

3. Physical Stress:

• Description: Physical stress is connected to circumstances that impact the body, such as disease, injury, or lack of sleep.
Example: Recovering from surgery, suffering from chronic pain, or enduring sleep deprivation.

4. Emotional Stress:

• Description: Emotional stress occurs from events that generate powerful emotions, such as grief, rage, fear, or frustration. Example: Dealing with a breakup, coping with grief, or managing interpersonal issues.

5. Environmental Stress:

• Description: Environmental stress originates from external elements in one's environment, such as noise, pollution, or congested living circumstances.

Example: Working in a noisy workplace, living in a polluted location, or encountering continual interruptions in the environment.

6. Workplace Stress:

• Description: Workplace stress is particular to job-related pressures and responsibilities, including tight deadlines, excessive workloads, and interpersonal problems.

Example: Juggling several duties, coping with a demanding boss, or managing a competitive work climate.

7. Financial Stress:

• Description: Financial stress stems from worry about money, budgeting, debt, or financial instability.

Example: Facing unemployment, battling debt, or handling unforeseen bills.

8. Post-Traumatic Stress:

• Description: Post-Traumatic Stress Disorder (PTSD) arises after exposure to a traumatic incident, producing enduring suffering and impairment in daily life.

Example: Surviving a natural disaster, experiencing battle, or being a victim of violence.

9. Cognitive Stress:

• Description: Cognitive stress is associated with mental processes and obstacles, such as excessive concern, perfectionism, or cognitive overload.

Example: Constantly concentrating on negative thoughts, creating unreasonable goals, or feeling overwhelmed by information.

10. Social Stress:

• Description: Social stress occurs from obstacles in interpersonal interactions, including disagreements with family, friends, or colleagues.

Example: Estrangement from family, managing societal expectations, or dealing with social isolation.

11. Routine Stress:

• Description: Routine stress is part of everyday life and encompasses routine inconveniences and annoyances people endure routinely.

Example: Traffic congestion, small hassles, or time strain in everyday duties.

12. Adaptive Stress:

• Description: Adaptive stress is a beneficial sort of stress that promotes development and adaptability. It can lead to enhanced resilience and improved coping abilities.

Example: Facing new difficulties, taking on responsibilities, or venturing outside one's comfort zone.

Understanding the many forms of stress assists individuals in recognizing the causes of stress in their lives and building effective coping techniques to manage and lessen its impact.

It's crucial to note that everyone feels stress differently, and what may be difficult for one person may not be the same for another.

Understanding Anxiety

Anxiety is a normal stress reaction marked by emotions of concern or uneasiness. While some amount of fear is acceptable and might be adaptive, excessive or persistent anxiety that interferes with everyday living may suggest an anxiety disorder.

The mind and body, inextricably interwoven, constitute a deep and symbiotic interaction that defines our well-being. This physiological relationship extends to emotions, thinking, and general health. This investigation of the mind-body link reveals the delicate aspects that characterizes our holistic life.

1. Understanding the Unity:

The mind-body link is not a notion; it's the substance of our existence. At its essence, this link represents the interconnectedness of mental and physical health.

Our ideas and emotions affect our physical condition; conversely, our physical well-being impacts our mental state. To comprehend one, we must appreciate the other.

2. The Power of Thoughts:

Our ideas are more than transitory happenings; they significantly influence physical health. Positive thoughts may initiate a cascade of neurochemical reactions that raise mood and increase general well-being. Conversely, persistent stress or negative thinking patterns may emerge physiologically, harming immunological function, cardiovascular health, and digestive systems.

3. Emotions as Messengers:

Emotions, sometimes called the language of the soul, are strong messages that cross the gap between mind and body. When we experience emotions, our body reacts with physiological changes. Stress, for instance, promotes the release of cortisol, influencing heart rate and blood pressure.

Understanding and controlling emotions is crucial to preserving balance within the mind-body relationship.

4. Stress and Relaxation Response:

The omnipresent presence of stress in everyday life highlights the relevance of the mind-body link.

Chronic stress not only burdens mental health but also manifests physically, leading to illnesses including muscular tightness, migraines, and reduced immunological function. Conversely, triggering the relaxation response via meditation and deep breathing supports physical and mental renewal.

5. Lifestyle Choices and Physical Health:

Daily choices, from diet to physical exercise, have a key influence on the mind-body link. A healthy diet feeds the body and brain, impacting cognitive performance and emotional well-being. Regular exercise strengthens the body and produces endorphins, the body's natural mood enhancers.

6. The Role of Mind-Body Practices:

Mind-body activities, ranging from yoga to mindfulness meditation, provide purposeful paths for developing harmony. These activities actively engage the mind and body, fostering relaxation, stress reduction, and heightened self-awareness. They become vehicles for better understanding the mind-body link and supporting general well-being.

7. Holistic Wellness:

In essence, the mind-body link underlines the comprehensive aspect of well-being. To obtain actual health, one must treat not just bodily problems but also dig into the realms of mental and emotional well-being. This holistic approach highlights the interdependence of all elements of our lives and encourages people to engage in their health journey actively.

As we travel the many paths of the mind-body connection, let us embrace the deep truth that our well-being is a harmonic symphony, where the mind and body dance together perfectly.

This inquiry urges us to comprehend and actively foster this link, unleashing the possibility for robust health and deep self-awareness.

Key Components of Anxiety

1. Excessive concern: Anxiety typically entails excessive, uncontrolled concern about future events or circumstances. The intensity and length of the anxiety might be disproportionate to the actual threat.

2. Bodily Symptoms: Anxiety can manifest in bodily symptoms, including muscular tension, restlessness, elevated heart rate, perspiration, and gastrointestinal distress.

3. Cognitive Symptoms: Anxious thoughts may include fear of the unknown, catastrophic thinking and a heightened sense of vulnerability. Individuals with anxiety may also have trouble concentrating and have indecisiveness.

4. Emotional Symptoms: Anxiety is accompanied by acute emotional experiences, such as feelings of dread, anger, and a sense of impending doom.

Types of Anxiety Disorders

Anxiety disorders span a variety of ailments, each with its distinct features and impact:

1. Generalized Anxiety Disorder (GAD): Characterized by persistent and excessive anxiety about numerous elements of life, GAD may be all-encompassing, impacting everyday functioning.

2. Panic Disorder: Intense and abrupt bouts of terror, known as panic attacks, may be accompanied by physical symptoms, including chest discomfort and shortness of breath.

3. Social Anxiety Disorder: Fear of social events and the scrutiny of others may lead to avoidance behavior and substantial discomfort.

4. Certain Phobias: Intense fear and avoidance of certain things or circumstances, such as heights or spiders, define specialized phobias.

Relationship Between Stress and Anxiety

• Stress as a Precursor to Anxiety: Prolonged or excessive stress can contribute to the development or worsening of anxiety disorders. Chronic stress may heighten the body's general susceptibility to stress, raising the chance of anxiety.

• Shared Physiological Responses: Both stress and anxiety trigger the body's stress response, resulting in comparable physiological changes. Chronic stimulation of this response can contribute to a state of heightened arousal associated with anxiety.

• Individual Differences: While stress is a typical cause of anxiety, not everyone who encounters stress develops an anxiety condition. Individual differences in coping methods, resilience, and other things play a role in the incidence and severity of anxiety symptoms.

• Coping skills: Effective stress management and coping skills can help decrease the impact of stress and lower the chance of developing anxiety. These may include mindfulness, relaxation methods, cognitive-behavioral therapy (CBT), and lifestyle adjustments.

• Treatment Approaches: Addressing stress and anxiety frequently takes a diverse approach. This may involve psychotherapy, medication, lifestyle modifications, and stress reduction approaches customized to the individual's unique requirements and circumstances.

In summary, stress is a natural response to difficulties, but anxiety comprises chronic and excessive concern and dread. Understanding the link between stress and anxiety is vital for establishing effective coping techniques and getting appropriate treatment when required. If stress or anxiety severely disrupts everyday functioning, obtaining help from mental health specialists is advised.

Effective coping methods for stress and anxiety

Coping with stress and anxiety entails adopting methods that help regulate emotions, lower physiological arousal, and build resilience.

Here are some practical coping strategies for stress and anxiety:

1. Mindfulness and Meditation:

Practice mindfulness. Engage in mindfulness activities to bring attention to the present moment. Deep breathing, guided meditation, and body scanning can help alleviate stress and anxiety.

2. Deep Breathing Exercises:

Diaphragmatic breathing: Practice deep breathing by inhaling steadily via your nose, allowing your diaphragm to enlarge, and expelling slowly through your mouth. This might stimulate the body's relaxing response.

3. Progressive Muscle Relaxation (PMR):

Tension-release technique: Systematically tighten and then release distinct muscle groups to achieve physical relaxation and reduce overall tension.

4. Cognitive-Behavioral Techniques (CBT):

Identify and challenge negative ideas. Recognize and confront unreasonable or negative beliefs that contribute to stress and anxiety. Replace them with more balanced and good-minded people.

5. Expressive Writing:

Journaling: Write down your ideas and emotions. This can bring clarity, assist in processing feelings, and act as a therapeutic release for stress.

6. Physical Activity:

Regular exercise: Participate in regular exercise to release endorphins, which function as natural mood boosters. Walking, running, yoga, or dancing might be helpful.

7. Social Support:

Connect with others: Share your feelings with trustworthy friends, relatives, or a support network. Social Support may bring comfort, perspective, and a sense of belonging.

8. Time Management:

Prioritize tasks: Break tasks into smaller chunks and prioritize them. Setting realistic objectives and managing time properly help lessen feelings of overload.

9. Relaxation Techniques:

Guided imagery: Use guided imagery or visualization to generate a relaxing mental image, helping to reduce tension and promote relaxation.

Healthy Lifestyle Choices

- Balanced diet: Maintain a well-balanced and nutritious diet to support overall physical and mental well-being.
- Adequate sleep: Ensure sufficient and quality sleep since rest significantly influences stress and anxiety levels.

- Self-Compassion: Be gentle with yourself. Practice self-compassion and avoid self-critical thoughts. Treat yourself with the same kindness you would provide to a friend.

- Set Boundaries: Learn to say no. Establish clear limits and learn to say no when required. Overcommitting can cause stress.

- Mindful Activities: Engage in hobbies. Participate in activities you like, whether reading, gardening, painting, or any other interest that gives relaxation and delight.

- Professional Support:
Therapy: Consider pursuing therapy or counselling to examine deeper issues and acquire more coping methods.

- Cognitive-behavioral therapy (CBT) is beneficial for stress and anxiety. It's crucial to remember that successful coping tactics may differ from person to person, and various strategies could be most helpful.

Additionally, obtaining expert help from a mental health professional can provide specialized direction and support tailored to your unique needs and circumstances.

Building resilience in the face of life's adversities

Building resilience is vital for overcoming life's obstacles and rebounding from hardship. Resilience entails developing the capacity to adapt, cope with stress, and grow in adversity. Here are techniques to improve stability:

1. Cultivate a Positive Mindset:

Optimism: Focus on the good elements of situations and create an optimistic mindset. Challenge negative thinking and search for silver linings even in complex circumstances.

2. Develop Strong Social Connections:

Build a Support System: Foster meaningful ties with friends, family, and the community. Having a solid support system gives emotional comfort during challenging times.

3. Practice Self-Care:

prioritize Well-Being: Take care of your physical and mental health via regular exercise, a good diet, and sufficient sleep. Self-care helps with overall resilience.

4. Maintain Flexibility:

Adaptability: Develop the ability to adjust to changing situations. Being adaptable in your ideas and approach might help you tackle unanticipated problems more efficiently.

5. Learn problem-solving skills:

Critical Thinking: Enhance your problem-solving abilities and approach difficulties with a solution-focused perspective. Break difficulties into achievable stages and strive towards solutions.

6. Develop Emotional Regulation:

Regulate Emotions: Learn to detect and regulate your emotions successfully. Developing emotional control abilities helps you manage stress and retain composure.

7. Build Coping Mechanisms:

Good Coping Strategies: Identify and practice suitable coping methods for stress, such as mindfulness, relaxation techniques, or engaging in activities that offer joy and relaxation.

8. Set realistic goals:

Achievable Objectives: Set reasonable and achievable goals. Break major ambitions into smaller, doable activities. Celebrate minor triumphs along the way.

9. Cultivate Gratitude:

Thankfulness Practice: Focus on the good parts of your life and create a sense of thankfulness. Keeping a thankfulness notebook might help transform your outlook.

10. Develop a Sense of Purpose:

Meaningful Activities: Engage in activities that offer your life purpose and significance. Having a sense of purpose can bring drive and perseverance in challenging circumstances.

11. Practice Mindfulness:

Present Moment Awareness: Embrace mindfulness methods to stay present in the moment. Mindfulness can reduce stress and boost your capacity to cope with obstacles.

12. Build Confidence and Self-Efficacy:

Positive Self-Talk: Cultivate positive self-talk and beliefs about your abilities to overcome obstacles. Building self-confidence adds to resilience.

13. Seek Support:

Professional Help: Get treatment from mental health specialists if needed. Therapy can give valuable insights and coping methods for facing life's obstacles.

14. Learn from Adversity:

Resilience as a Skill: View hardship as an opportunity for growth and learning. Reflect on prior obstacles and evaluate how you've effectively overcome them.

Building resilience is a continual process that requires deliberate work and a readiness to pick up new skills and adapt.

Adopting these tactics into your life will boost your capacity to manage stress, bounce back from setbacks, and create a more resilient mentality.

CHAPTER 5

CONCLUSION

In the comprehensive investigation of "Mind Matters: Navigating the Landscape of Mental Well-Being," the intricate interplay between numerous elements impacting mental health has come to the forefront. The diverse structure of the mind's topography incorporates emotional intelligence, stress management, and resilience as major components, each playing a significant part in molding our mental well-being.

Emotional intelligence, a cornerstone of understanding and regulating emotions, helps individuals build self-awareness, manage emotional reactions, and establish meaningful connections. This heightened emotional awareness adds significantly to mental resilience, assisting individuals in adjusting to life's adversities more easily.

Stress management is a vital feature in the landscape of mental well-being. The realization that stress is a natural part of life, along with adequate coping methods, helps individuals handle stress without succumbing to persistent or overwhelming demands.

Strategies such as mindfulness, deep breathing, and positive reframing give vital tools to manage stress and flourish in the face of adversity.
The capacity for resilience, or overcoming adversity, is
a beacon of strength in the mental health landscape. It entails establishing a positive outlook, adjusting to change, and perceiving problems as chances for progress. By accepting that failures are a normal part of the human experience, individuals may use resilience to overcome difficulties and emerge stronger.

Lifestyle choices and social interactions thread themselves delicately into the fabric of mental well-being. Adopting a holistic approach that includes regular exercise, a balanced diet, appropriate sleep, and meaningful social contacts adds to the general health of the mind.

Social Support, a cornerstone of mental well-being, underlines the need to develop relationships with others, break down social stigmas, and provide a supportive atmosphere where individuals feel understood and respected.

As we travel the landscape of mental well-being, it becomes evident that the mind is still in the more excellent environment of our lives. It is closely linked to our relationships, jobs, and daily experiences. Breaking down mental and physical health barriers, recognizing the symbiotic link between the two, and cultivating a culture of open communication and understanding are critical steps in establishing a society where the mind matters truly counts.

In conclusion, "Mind Matters" serves as a sobering reminder that the investigation of mental well-being is a continuous

and social adventure. By delving into the complexities of our minds, being aware of the elements that affect mental health, and embracing a holistic and compassionate approach, we pave the way for a society where individuals can navigate the landscape of their minds with resilience, empathy and a profound commitment to well-being.

www.ingramcontent.com/pod-product-compliance
Lightning Source LLC
Chambersburg PA
CBHW070820280726
48660CB00016B/2147